FOUND ALPHABET

Houghton Mifflin Company,
215 Park Avenue South, New York, New York 10003.

www.houghtonmifflinbooks.com

The text of this book is set in Triplex.
The illustrations are arranged found objects.

Library of Congress Cataloging-in-Publication Data

Shindler, Ramon.
Found alphabet / by Ramon Shindler and Wojciech Graniczewski ;
illustrations by Anita Andrzejewska and Andrzej Pilichowski-Ragno.
p. cm.
Summary: Rhyming text and illustrations created with various found objects
introduce the letters of the alphabet.
ISBN 0-618-44232-4
[1. Alphabet. 2. Stories in rhyme.]   I. Graniczewski, Wojciech.   II. Andrzejewska,
Anita, ill. III. Pilichowski-Ragno, Andrezej, ill. IV. Title.
    PZ8.3.S5563Fo 2005
    [E]—dc22   2004009464
ISBN-13: 978-0618-44232-4

Printed in Singapore
TWP 10 9 8 7 6 5 4 3 2 1

FOUND
ALPHABET

Written by
Ramon Shindler
and
Wojciech Graniczewski

Illustrations by **Anita Andrzejewska** and **Andrzej Pilichowski-Ragno**

Houghton Mifflin Company • **Boston 2005**

A

Here's an airplane in the sky
It doesn't need to fly so high

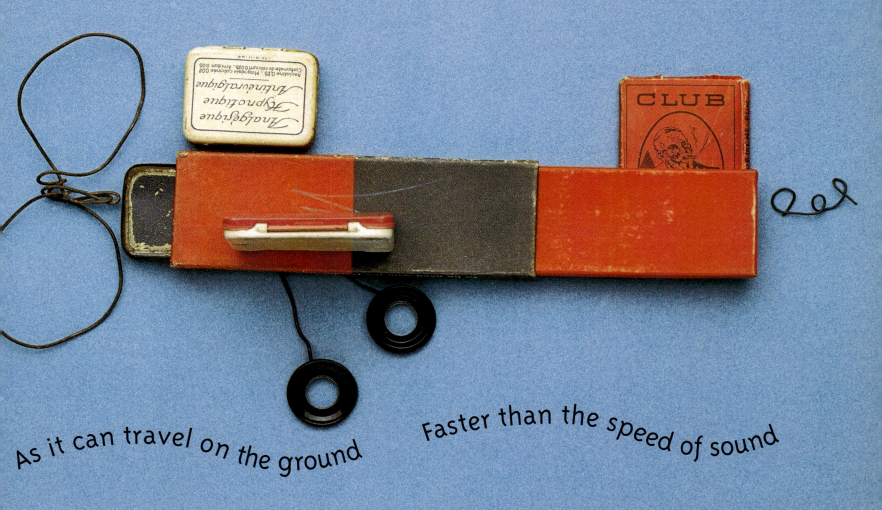

As it can travel on the ground   Faster than the speed of sound

B

Butterfly, butterfly!
You're not flying—
tell me why!

"My wings of bread cannot fly

Without butter they get dry"

C

If you want to travel far
Get yourself a clockwork car

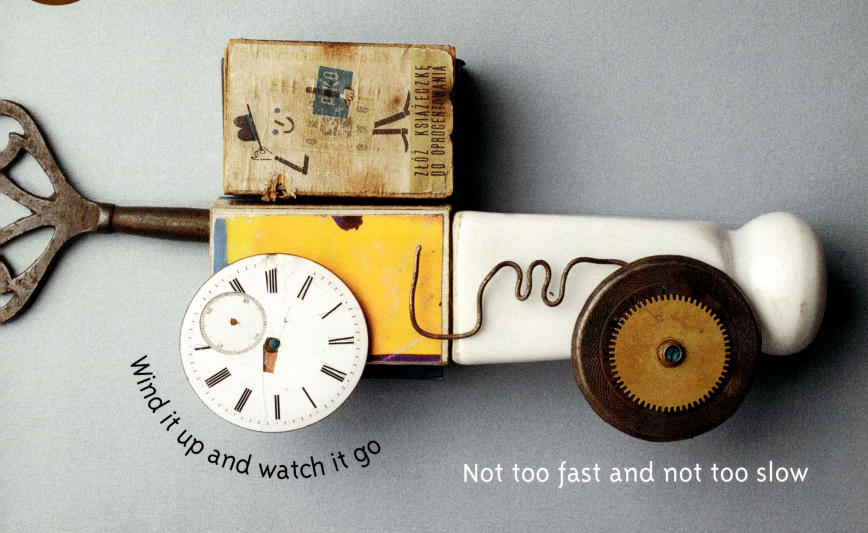

Wind it up and watch it go

Not too fast and not too slow

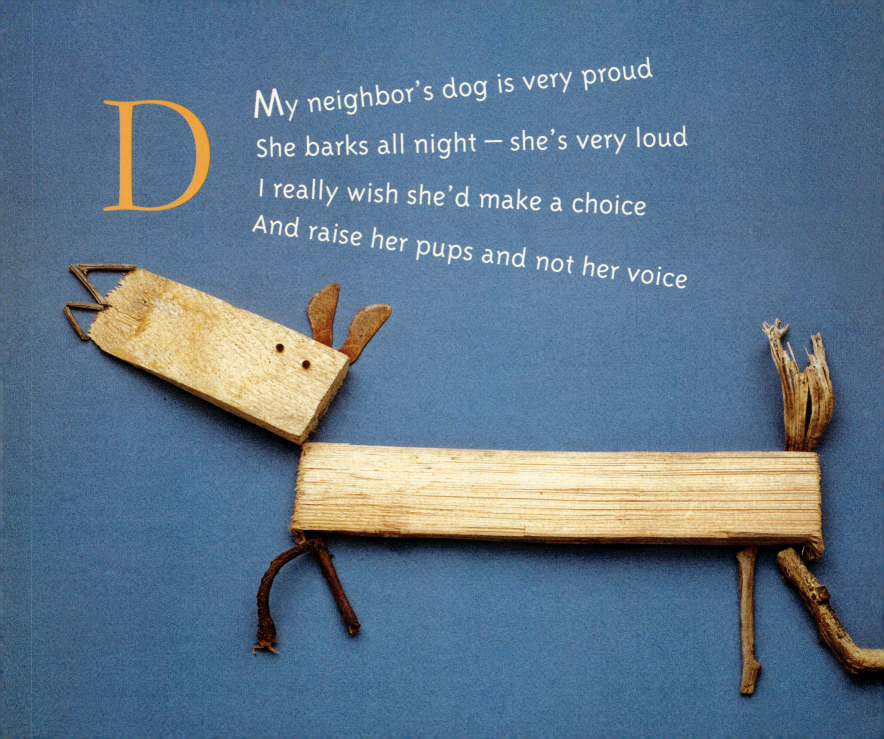

D

My neighbor's dog is very proud
She barks all night — she's very loud
I really wish she'd make a choice
And raise her pups and not her voice

E

This railroad engine, strong and tough
Is full of steam and full of puff
While racing here
through fog and rain
It stayed on track
but lost its train

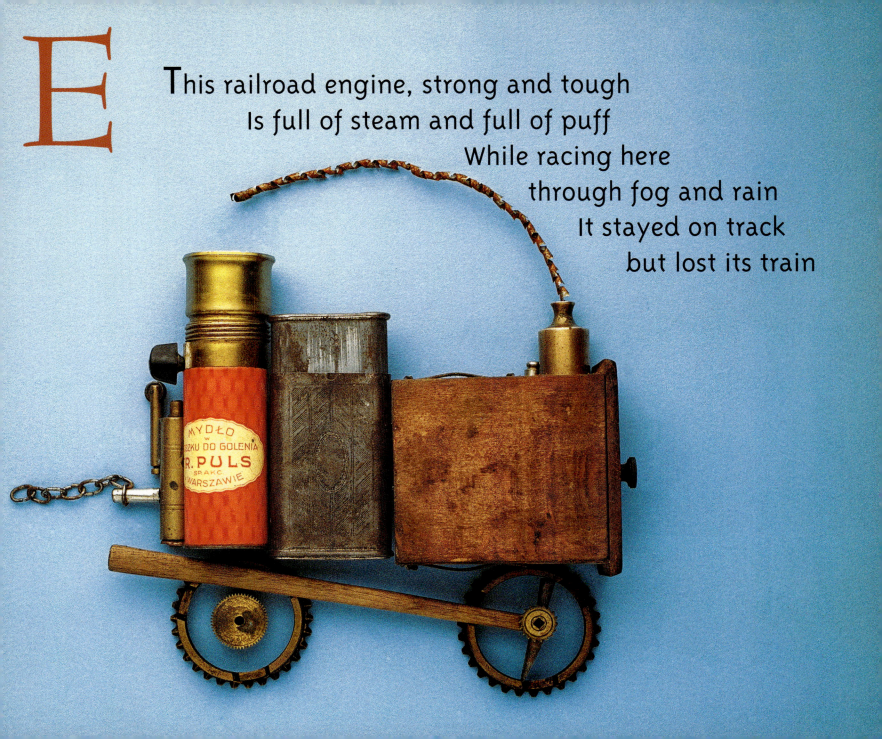

F

When you meet this magic fish
Close your eyes and make a wish
This will make your dreams come true
Not all of them, just one or two

G

Let's do something for a laugh
And play a game with this giraffe
But don't forget
      she's rather tall
I bet she's good
      at basketball

H

This little house
is on our block
The key is always
in the lock

So if you need
a place to hide
Just turn it once
and go inside

I'd like to be an Eskimo
And have an igloo made of snow
I built this one and keep it neat
My dentist thinks it's much too sweet

J

Jack-in-the-box is this guy's name
And scaring people is his game
He comes in lots of shapes and sizes
Tightly packed to spring surprises

K

While I was diving in the sea
I came across this ancient key
You can rent it on request
If you find the treasure chest

L

This reading lamp
  hangs by my bed
Upon the wall
  behind my head
It's on all day
  and off all night
As you can see
  it's not too bright

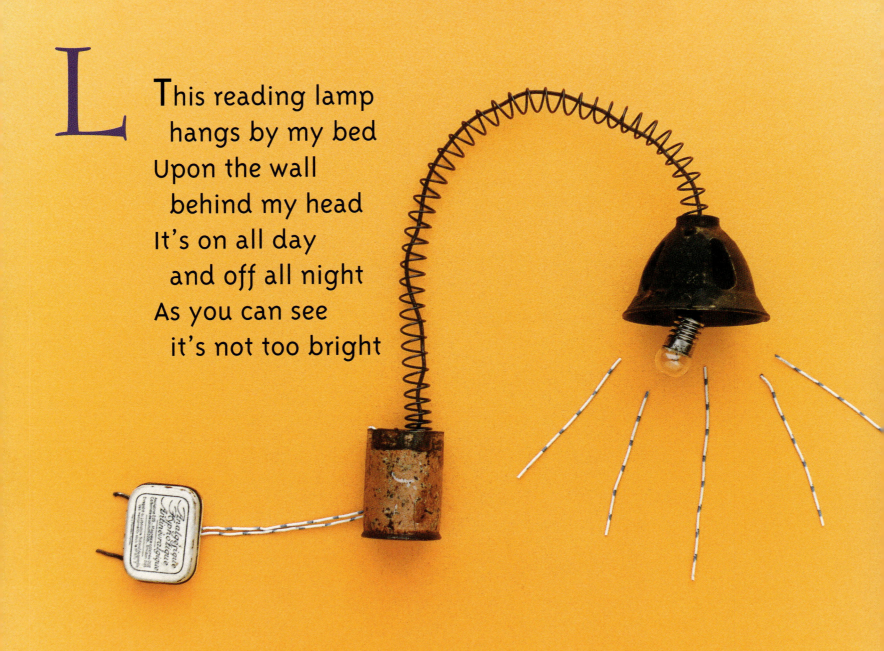

M

This silver mouse is made of tin
She's very strong though rather thin

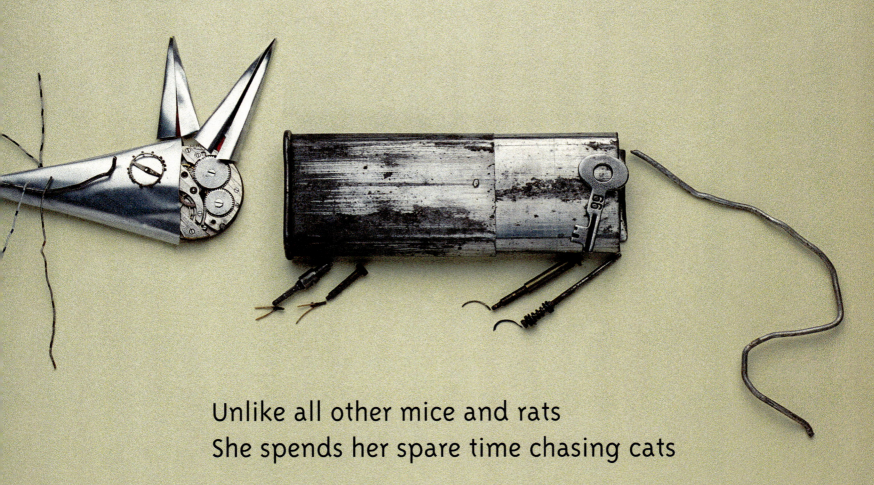

Unlike all other mice and rats
She spends her spare time chasing cats

N

Look at this bird! Perhaps you've guessed
What he's doing in this nest
He's waiting there, I have a hunch
For mom to come back with his lunch

This octopus has many charms
She'll welcome you with open arms
But just beware, she's quite a flirt
Don't get too close or you'll get hurt

P

My parrot is
a talking bird
"Hello" is her
favorite word
My cat and dog
suggest I try
To teach her how
to say "goodbye"

Q

This queen gets lonely
on her throne
And often when
she's all alone
She puts on jeans,
takes off her crown
Hops on a bus
and goes to town

R

This noisy rhino is unfair
He lives upstairs and doesn't care
I told him twice to show some feeling
But still he dances on my ceiling

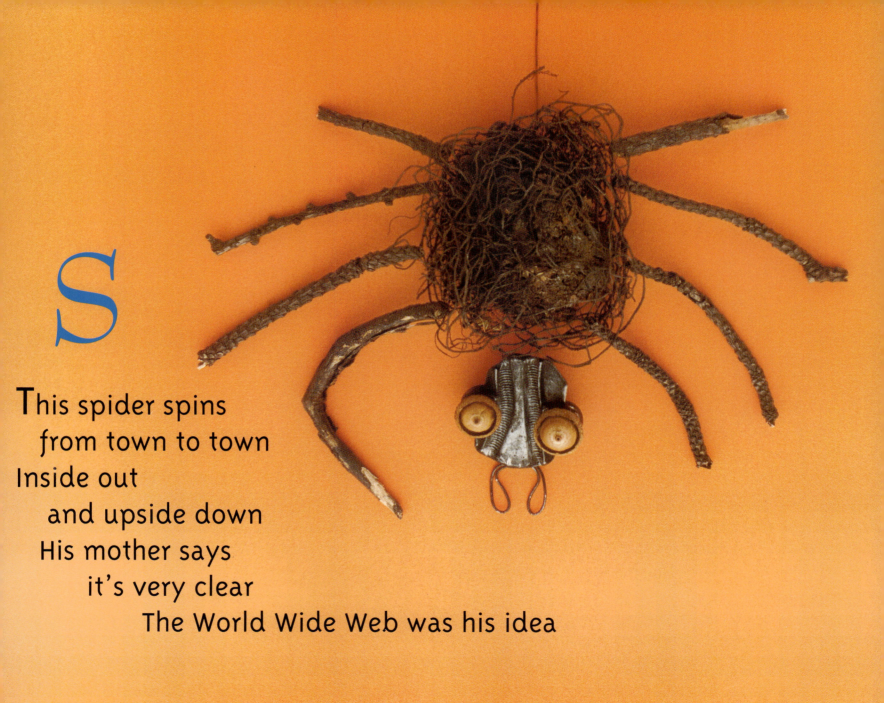

S

This spider spins
  from town to town
Inside out
  and upside down
  His mother says
    it's very clear
      The World Wide Web was his idea

T

This train flies just above the track
It goes nowhere and then comes back
You'll never ever have to wait
Despite the fact it's always late

U

One day while in
my granddad's cellar
I came across this
strange umbrella

When autumn leaves began to *fall*
It didn't keep me dry at all

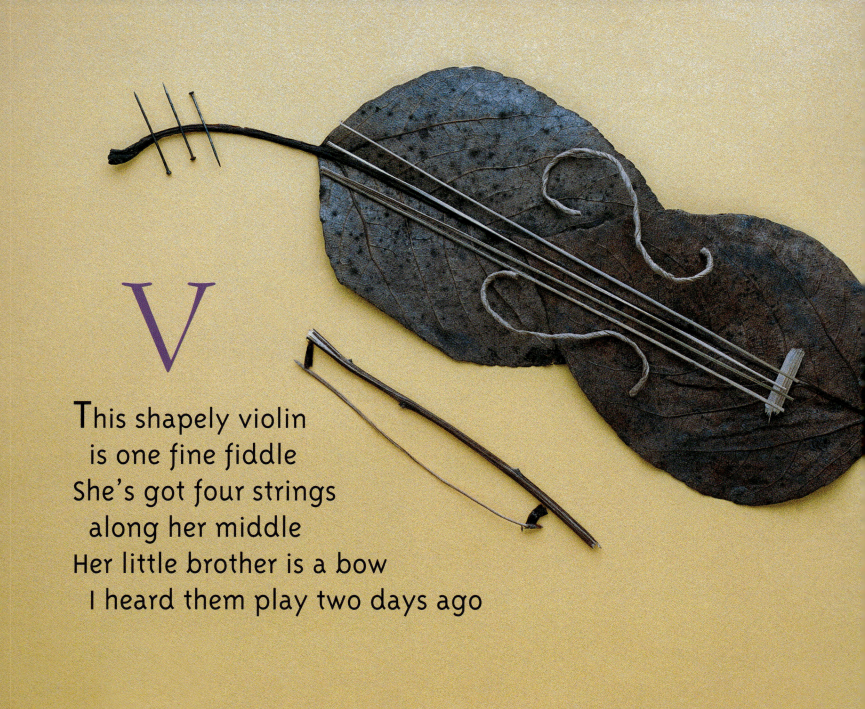

V

This shapely violin
  is one fine fiddle
She's got four strings
  along her middle
Her little brother is a bow
  I heard them play two days ago

W

This wolf is quite a scary sight
His long, sharp teeth are sparkling white
I'm sure he'd eat you if he could
He can't because he's made of wood

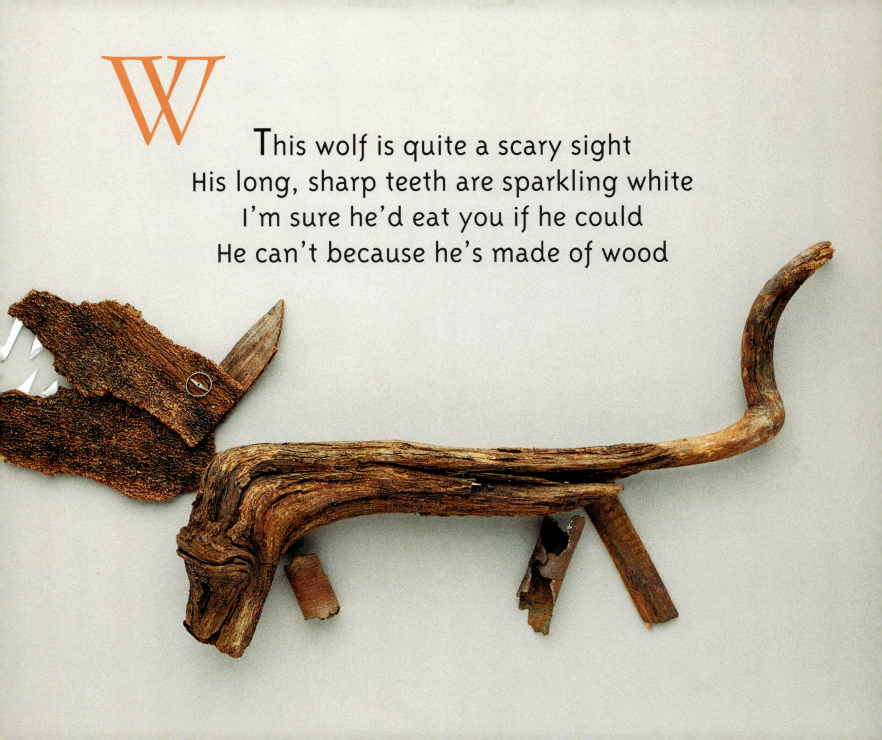

X

Now try to guess and tell me why

An x-ray camera needs no eye

Because no matter what you do   It always simply sees through you

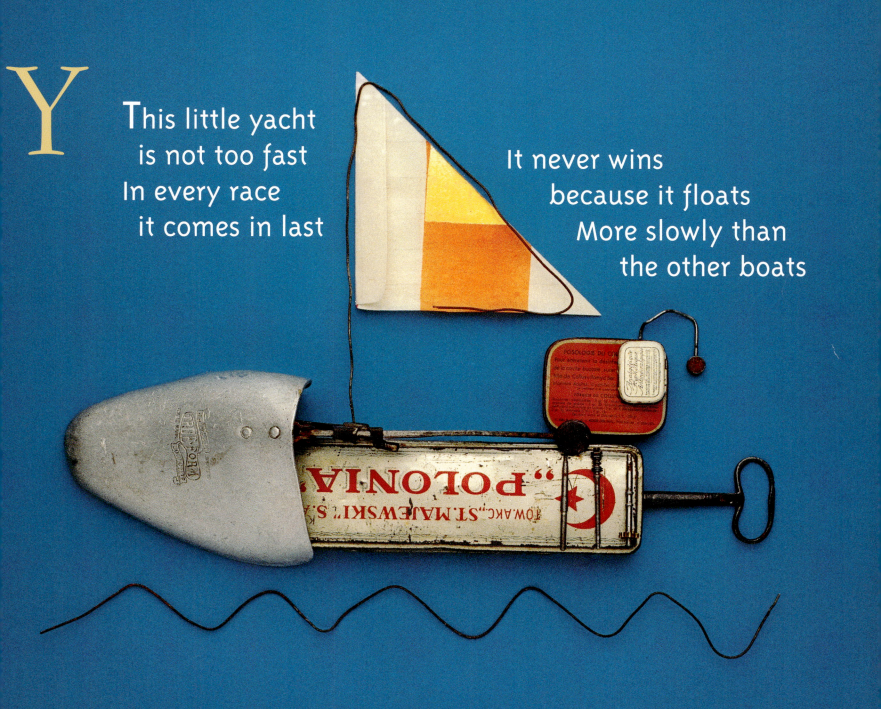

Y

This little yacht
is not too fast
In every race
it comes in last

It never wins
because it floats
More slowly than
the other boats

Z

Look at this zebra dressed in stripes
Of different colors, shapes, and types
While on her neck they're white and black
They're black and white across her back

A Note from the Creators of
FOUND ALPHABET

It was a hot Sunday afternoon, and so we went for a walk. As we strolled across a field we noticed some old oak trees. We decided to sit down and rest. We looked up at the rays of the sun shining through the branches. Then we saw an old house. We closed our eyes and went inside. The house was very interesting. It had lots of rooms linked by long hallways. Its winding stairways led to dark cellars and a large attic. And everywhere there were treasures, large and small. Nuts and bolts, chains and ropes, leaves and sticks, rings and cogs. And pieces of wood, and tin of different shapes and sizes. We started to put them together in different combinations. We made an airplane, a butterfly, a car, and lots, lots more. In fact, we made one for every letter of the alphabet. We then met a couple of wandering poets. We showed them what we had made. They looked at each other and immediately started to compose rhymes. One for each of the pictures. They said, "Just as you take objects and put them together to make pictures, we take words and put them together to make poems." We said, "You create pictures with your poems." They said, "You make poems with your pictures." And then we realized that we all live in the house of our imagination.

The four creators of **Found Alphabet** reside in Krakow, Poland. This is their first book published in the United States.

Anita Andrzejewska and **Andrzej Pilichowski-Ragno** are freelance artists who have worked together on several illustration projects. They created the art for **Found Alphabet** before the text was written. The art was meant to "inspire children to create new objects from useless wastes of natural materials, like wood, stone, paper, metal, and feathers, and reveal the beauty of these simple materials."

Ramon Shindler has spent many years traveling around the world as a teacher and teacher trainer. **Wojciech Graniczewski** spent many years traveling around the world with a theater company, for which he was an actor, a scriptwriter, and a director. Their paths crossed in the magic city of Krakow, where they now write TV scripts, songs, poems, and stories.